KW-482-417

Nanny

Alfie

Star

Rosie

Dear Jack,

My little storyteller!

As you know, the family is going to be setting up camp on a new site very soon. We'll probably be staying there for a while, because Farmer Jenkins says there's going to be lots of work for your dad, mum, aunts and uncles. And this has given me a wonderful idea – I'm giving you and your three cousins diaries to write in. That way, you won't have to spend so much time remembering your childhoods when you're old like I am. You'll have already written them down!

You'll notice that, unlike your cousins, I've given you an _extra_ book. That's because I know that, if I didn't, you'd use this one for your brilliant drawings, and your exciting stories. I reckon that one day, lots and lots of people are going to want to read them.

Love,

Nanny

The Caravan Diaries

JACK'S DIARY!

Written by Jimmy Noble
Illustrated by Gareth Williams

HODDER
Education

Hachette UK's policy is to use papers that are natural, renewable and recyclable products and made from wood grown in well-managed forests and other controlled sources. The logging and manufacturing processes are expected to conform to the environmental regulations of the country of origin.

ISBN: 978 1 3983 7707 3

Text © Jimmy Noble
Design, illustrations and layout © 2023 Hodder & Stoughton Limited

First published in 2023 by Hodder & Stoughton Limited (for its Hodder Education imprint, part of the Hodder Education Group),

An Hachette UK Company
Carmelite House, 50 Victoria Embankment, London EC4Y 0DZ,

www.hoddereducation.com

Impression number 10 9 8 7 6 5 4 3 2 1
Year 2027 2026 2025 2024 2023

Author: Jimmy Noble
Series Editor: Catherine Coe
Commissioning Editor: Hamish Baxter
Educational Consultant: Pauline Allen
Illustrators: Gareth Williams/Advocate Art (Map by Barking Dog Art and
    Family Photo by Sarah Lawrence/Advocate Art)
Design concept: Lynda Murray
Page layout: Rocket Design (East Anglia) Ltd
Editorial: Iolanda Steadman

With thanks to the schools that took part in the development of *Reading Planet* KS2, including: Ancaster CE Primary School, Ancaster; Downsway Primary School, Reading; Ferry Lane Primary School, London; Foxborough Primary School, Slough; Griffin Park Primary School, Blackburn; St Barnabas CE First & Middle School, Pershore; Tranmoor Primary School, Doncaster; and Wilton CE Primary School, Wilton.

A catalogue record for this title is available from the British Library.

Printed in the UK.

Orders: Please contact Hachette UK Distribution, Hely Hutchinson Centre, Milton Road, Didcot, Oxfordshire, OX11 7HH.
Telephone: +44 (0)1235 400555. Email: primary@hachette.co.uk.

MIX
Paper | Supporting
responsible forestry
FSC™ C104740

GYPSY JOHN

The world's only Gypsy superhero!

John can see for miles and miles

John can fly

John can run faster than a car

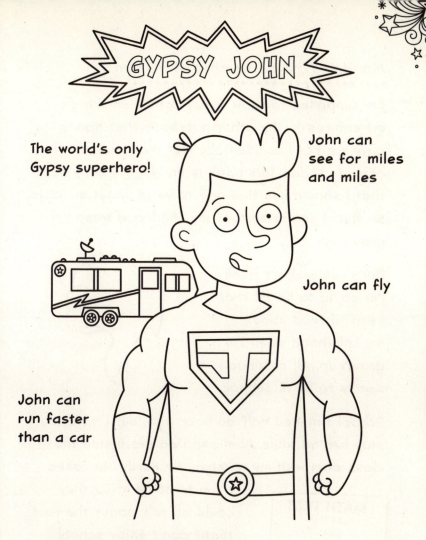

He's incredibly strong <u>but</u> ...

he sometimes gets tired of having to carry his caravan lair from place to place.

OOPS! I'm writing in the wrong book!

Monday 22nd September. 4:00 p.m.

I'm supposed to draw Gypsy John's amazing adventures in the other notebook that Nanny gave me but I accidentally left that back at the caravan today. This book is my <u>diary</u>. Nanny says that I should use this one to write about my days, so that I can remember my childhood when I'm grown up.

But I really don't think I'm going to be all that keen to read about my childhood when I'm grown up. All childhood seems to be is <u>school</u>!

School finished half an hour ago, but I have to stay behind while Mum and Dad are inside the classroom with my teacher, Mr Hardy. He asked them to come in so they could all talk about the fact that I don't enjoy school very much.

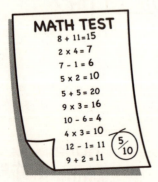

MATH TEST
8 + 11 = 15
2 x 4 = 7
7 - 1 = 6
5 x 2 = 10
5 + 5 = 20
9 x 3 = 16
10 - 6 = 4
4 x 3 = 10
12 - 1 = 11
9 + 2 = 11

5/10

I also did badly in a maths test last week, and he wants to discuss that, too.

I'm not like my older cousin, Alfie, who is living with us on Farmer Jenkins's land. He's always enjoyed going to school. He likes learning, and he's good at sports. I don't join in the sports at break time, because I don't want my classmates to laugh at how rubbish I am (and I don't think I would be picked, anyway).

Who tried to charge their phone!?

I also can't really join in when the other kids chat about the shows they love because I don't get to watch much TV at the camp. Whenever we have too many plugs on at the same time, all the caravans lose power.

If I got to do more drawing at school, I would enjoy it more, but we rarely get to do drawing. We spend most of our time on boring lessons.

Monday 22nd September. 5:00 p.m.

Mum and Dad weren't in the classroom very long. Mum smiled at me as they came out, but it wasn't a proper smile. It looked <u>sad</u>.

Back at the camp, they took me inside our caravan and sat me down at the table. They told me that Mr Hardy had said, "Jack is well behaved, but he needs to speak up when he doesn't understand something."

Now I knew what had been wrong with Mum's smile. I asked if they were upset with me. They both said no, and Dad reached across the table to ruffle my hair. He said I should not be scared of letting the teacher know when I needed help during lessons.

I stared at the table for a few seconds. I felt like I might cry until Dad said, "Some people need a bit of help at school, and that's OK."

Tuesday 23rd September. 4:00 p.m.

I was feeling miserable when I went to bed last night. I felt like my parents were disappointed in me, even though they said they weren't. When I woke up, I told myself that I was going

to start raising my hand in class. I was going to

ask Mr Hardy to explain things I didn't understand. And when I knew the answer to something, I would speak up and say it.

There was just one problem with this plan ... Isaac! He sits next to me in class, and sticks his hand up for <u>every</u> question, even when he doesn't know the answer!

Today, Mr Hardy was teaching us our 12 times tables, and he asked me, "What is 3 x 12?" I always get hot in the face when he asks me questions. I looked down at the table, thinking hard until I worked out the answer.

But just as I looked up, Isaac was raising his hand so high he was practically floating out of his chair. He shouted, "36! 36! 36!"

Mr Hardy said that he had wanted me to answer.

"Jack was taking too long," Isaac said. My cheeks and ears were very hot now, and I looked back down at the table while Mr Hardy calmly told Isaac to let others have a chance at answering a question sometimes.

I stayed quiet for the rest of the lesson, even when I really needed help understanding something. I knew Mum and Dad had said it was OK to ask for help sometimes, but I didn't want my classmates to get annoyed because Mr Hardy kept on having to explain the same things again and again.

The bell rang to tell us it was lunchtime. I began putting my pencil case in my bag.

Isaac leaned over and grabbed my bag. "Is that a comic?" he wanted to know.

I realised that I had not put my comic book back at the bottom of my bag like I usually do. Isaac had seen the picture of Gypsy John on the cover and was starting to reach for it. I snatched my bag back from him. "Don't chore* it!" I said.

Isaac looked confused and said he only wanted to look at it.

I didn't say anything. Everyone in the classroom had stopped what they were doing. They were staring at us. At <u>me</u>. I zipped up my bag, stood up from my chair and slunk out of the classroom. I had been planning on asking if I could play football with Isaac and the others during lunchtime, but I thought Isaac probably didn't like me very much after that.

* 'Chore' = one of Nanny's words. It means 'steal'.

I ate my sandwich as quickly as I could. Since I wasn't playing football at lunch, I decided to use the time to draw, which I preferred to

playing football, anyway. I had an awesome idea for the next villain Gypsy John could fight ...

Luke Loud!

Luke is a real mouthy mush. His voice can be heard hundreds of miles away, and he can shatter the windows of John's caravan lair just by shouting.

I couldn't wait to draw their fights but I had no idea how Gypsy John could overcome Luke Loud. All Luke had to do was talk, and Gypsy John would have to cover his ears. Then Luke could swoop in and <u>bosh</u>!

Gypsy John would be in real trouble!

I still hadn't figured it out by the time lunch was over.

* 'Mush' (rhymes with 'push') = 'man'.

Tuesday 23rd September. 8:00 p.m.

I'm sitting in my caravan. I did some more drawings after dinner, but I <u>still</u> haven't worked out how Gypsy John can defeat Luke Loud.

Rosie came into the cook-hut*, where I was writing my last diary entry. She's the oldest of the cousins at the camp, and one of my favourite people. She plonked herself down next to me and asked if I was OK. She said that she'd overheard my parents talking in the caravan about their meeting with Mr Hardy.

I felt tears sting my eyes again. "I wish I wasn't shy," I told her.

"You should believe in yourself," Rosie said.

"But what if the other kids laugh at me for not understanding something that they think is simple?"

Rosie shook her head and smiled. "People aren't all that mean, Jack," she said.

* The cook-hut is where we all sit most of the time. We cook our dinners on the fire!

13

But Rosie wasn't living with
us last year. She didn't see
the kids at my last school
make fun of me for not
being able to do sums as
quickly as them. I don't
want that to happen again.
I'm not as brave as Gypsy John.

Then I remembered that I <u>did</u> get the answer
right today. Isaac might not have let me say it,
but I <u>did</u> work out that 3 x 12 = 36. All by myself!
If Mr Hardy asks me a question tomorrow, I might
know the answer to that one too.

Maybe I <u>don't</u> have to be
so scared of speaking up
in class. I'm going to go to
bed now, because I'm feeling
a bit tired.

Tuesday 23rd September. 8:30 p.m.
●●●●●●●●●●●●●●●●●●●●●●●●●●●●●●●

I've just figured out how Gypsy John can defeat Luke Loud ...

cotton wool!

I was nearly asleep when I remembered one of the annoying things about sleeping in a caravan. Sometimes, <u>earwigs</u> get inside, so Nanny says to put cotton wool in our ears while we sleep. It keeps the creepy-crawlies out, but it's hard to hear your alarm in the morning.

Gypsy John can stuff his ears with cotton wool so that Luke Loud's voice won't hurt so much. I bet Luke Loud will be <u>devastated</u> when he can't hurt John with his voice.

I was about to start drawing the fight in my comic book, but Mum has told me to go to sleep. There's no way I'll sleep now though — I'm too excited!

Wednesday 24th September. 8:30 a.m.

I decided to get to school early today so I could do more drawings before registration. The classroom would be quiet, and I'd be able to concentrate — until my classmates started turning up.

Isaac was the first to arrive. I put my comic back in my bag as soon as he walked through the door because I remembered how keen he was to see it yesterday. He didn't seem to be interested this morning, though. He seemed more concerned with setting up the lunchtime football match against Year 4.

I felt a tingle of hope in my chest. I wondered if Isaac would let me play. Then I felt a prickle of nerves — Year 3 vs Year 4 is always a very <u>big</u> deal. Everyone takes it really seriously, and I started worrying that I'd miss a winning goal — or let one in — and get blamed for Year 3 losing.

Wednesday 24th September. 1:00 p.m.

I didn't need to worry about being blamed for Year 3 losing.

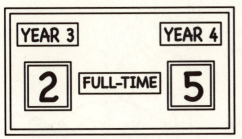

I waited all morning for Isaac to ask me to play, but he hadn't by the time the bell rang for lunch.

I remembered that Rosie said people weren't mean, so I hurried into the playground and stood at the edge of the huddle while Isaac was picking the Year 3 team. I tapped him on the shoulder and asked if he needed an extra player.

He looked confused. "We have all the players we need, Jack," he said.

I said, "Cool," like it was cool, but my face was hot as I trudged off towards the school building and back to our empty classroom.

I started drawing in my comic book. I'd got to the bit in my story where Gypsy John laughs as Luke Loud discovers that his words couldn't hurt him anymore. And then ...

Wednesday 24th September. 4:00 p.m.

I stopped the last entry because someone was calling for help in the playground. I rushed outside and saw everyone crowded around Isaac. He was trying to stand, but fell to the ground and clutched his  leg. He cried out and said he was scared it was broken. Mia, a girl in Year 4, was saying sorry for tackling him.

Isaac's dad came to the school to take him to the hospital. We all trooped back to the classroom after lunch. No one said anything. Mr Hardy said that Isaac might be kept home from school for a few days while his leg heals. Everyone looked at each other when he said that. Isaac really likes school. He's going to be fed up if he is stuck at home all day.

I know he always has to answer every question, but I feel sorry for him. I hope he's OK.

Thursday 25th September. 4:30 p.m.

It was extremely quiet in class today without Isaac. Everyone else got to answer questions. But I still didn't stick my hand up, not even when Mr Hardy asked if anyone knew how to spell 'treasure' — and I knew the answer to that.

At the end of the day, Mr Hardy looked right at me and asked if I would drop off some homework at Isaac's house after school tomorrow.

"Why me?" I asked him, confused.

Mr Hardy explained, "You're the only one in class who passes Isaac's house on their way home. Ask your parents tonight if it will be OK."

I jogged all the way back to the camp, because I wanted to do more drawings before dinner. But I've not been able to concentrate. I'm nervous about visiting Isaac.

I'm really not sure he'll want to see me.

Friday 26th September. 5:00 p.m.

I <u>knew</u> that wouldn't go very well!

I've just got back to the camp late. The parents are still in the fields working because it rained after lunchtime. Whenever that happens, they end up staying later, so they can pick all the apples they need to for the day. Nanny and Star are in

Nanny's caravan, making dinner for everyone. Rosie has taken her horse, Ruby, for a walk, and Alfie is in the field, practicing his kick-ups.

This means I have the cook-hut all to myself so I can write about my day. I don't think Nanny meant for any of us to fill our diaries with bad memories, but I can't help it. Today was awful!

I agreed to take Isaac's homework to him after school. Mr Hardy said that was very good of me, which was exactly what Isaac's mum said when I turned up at their house.

She showed me upstairs to Isaac's room. He was sitting on his bed, reading a football magazine. He had an elastic bandage around his foot, and he was resting the foot on top of a pile of pillows. I asked

him if he had a sprained ankle. He nodded. Then he asked, "What are you doing here?"

"He's come to bring you your homework and see you, sweetheart," his mum said. "Isn't that nice?"

Isaac looked like he didn't understand the question. "But we never really talk in school," he told her.

I flinched, worried that his mum would kick me out for pretending to be Isaac's friend. But she just said that she thought I was very good to 'make the effort'. Isaac didn't say anything. He just went back to his magazine.

I decided that I was probably going to gel on* pretty quickly.

* 'Gel on' = 'go', 'leave', 'get out of there'.

Isaac's mum said, "Maybe Jack would like to read the magazine with you?"

Isaac shook his head and said, "Jack doesn't like football."

"Well," said Isaac's mum, "maybe there's something else you can read together. I'll be downstairs. Shout if either of you needs anything." She turned to face me and put her hand on my shoulder as she whispered, "Thank you for coming to see him."

Isaac's mum went back downstairs. I took my bag off my shoulders and set it down on the floor so I could open it. I pulled out the exercise books Mr Hardy had asked me to give to Isaac so he could do the classwork the rest of us had been doing while he was away. There were so many, they almost fell out of my hands.

"Leave them next to my bed,"
Isaac said.

"How are you feeling?" I asked.

"Bored," he said, angrily
turning the page of his
magazine. "Wish I got to go to school."

I could not stop myself from laughing a little,
because that was the opposite of how I felt.
"Don't you like school?" he asked me.

"I don't like it as much as you seem to," I said.

He shrugged. "Maybe you'd like it more if you
studied harder."

I was starting to think visiting Isaac was a bad
idea. "I study as hard as everyone else," I said.

He looked up from his magazine. "So why do you
never know the answers to any questions?"

"I do sometimes know the
answers," I told him.
"I knew that 3 x 12 = 36."

He looked surprised and
confused. "Why didn't you answer
Mr Hardy, then?" he asked.

"Because you stuck your hand up, like you always do!" I shouted. I didn't mean to shout, but I couldn't understand why Isaac didn't get it. Didn't he realise that he should let other people talk from time to time?

I tried to keep my voice quiet as I said, "I just think you should let others speak sometimes. That would be a nice thing for you to do."

He still looked confused. "I'm nice to everyone," he said. "Everyone likes me."

"No, they just go along with whatever you want to do because you're bigger and louder than everyone else, so you always get your own way."

Isaac sat forward and glared at me. "You're just jealous because you don't have any friends!" he said.

I was now <u>sure</u> it had been a bad idea to visit Isaac. I snatched up my bag and marched out of his bedroom.

Isaac's mum met me at the front door. She looked very glum. "Isaac doesn't mean to upset anybody," she said.

I wanted to ask why Isaac didn't realise that telling someone they have no friends would upset them. But I just kept my eyes down as I left the house.

As soon as I was out, I ran all the way home to write in my diary. Now, I'm going to try to forget about what happened with Isaac and have some fun drawing.

Oh <u>no</u>!

I've just looked inside my bag and seen that my <u>comic book isn't there</u>. It must have got mixed up with the exercise books I gave to Isaac. This is terrible ...

Now I have to go <u>back</u> to Isaac's house!

Saturday 27th September. 7:30 a.m.

I was way too tired to write in my diary after I got back from Isaac's last night, so I've got up early today. I've come out to the cook-hut. I'm wearing a big jumper because mornings in the countryside can be very cold at this time of year. It's nice and quiet, though — no sounds are coming from any of the caravans, and I can't

even hear any cars in the distance. The only other person I've seen is Farmer Jenkins, who waved at me while he was taking his beagle, Archer, for a walk.

So, back to last night.

I was out of breath by the time I arrived at Isaac's house (I don't have as much energy as Gypsy John!). Isaac's mum seemed very confused

when I knocked at the door and told her I needed to speak to him again.

She let me in, and I went upstairs to Isaac's room. I pushed open the door without knocking.

Isaac was sitting on his bed, reading a book.

My comic book!

I ran into the room and snatched it back from him. "That's mine," I said. "I didn't say you could read it!"

He looked confused, like he couldn't understand why I would be upset that he was reading my private comic book. I started to feel frustrated with him. Why didn't he <u>understand</u>?

"I was only having a look," he said.

"You shouldn't look at things that aren't yours," I told him.

Isaac sat forward on his bed. "But ..."

"No, Isaac!" I said, stuffing the comic book into my bag. "You should respect other people's things."

Isaac frowned like he really didn't understand what I meant. He looked down at his hands for a moment. I could see his eyes narrow, like he was thinking hard. Then he looked up.

"I didn't mean to upset you, Jack," he said.

"OK, but you still shouldn't look at other people's things without permission," I said. I turned around and walked to the door. "I'll see you at school."

"It's brilliant, Jack," Isaac said. I stopped. "You're really good at drawing." This was the first time he had ever said anything nice to me. It felt strange at first, and I waited for him to say he was 'only joking'.

But he didn't. He just bounced a little on his bed. "Can you please show me what happens after Gypsy John catches up to Luke Loud?" he asked. "Please?"

I started to feel hot in the face again, but not from sadness this time. Now it was my shyness. I was as nervous as when Mr Hardy asked if anyone wanted to read aloud in class. But Isaac was sitting up in his bed, looking at me eagerly.

"Do you really want to know?" I asked him.

He nodded, his eyes very wide now. "I really, really do," he said. "John's got to figure out a way to stop Luke!"

I started smiling then. I'd always hoped someone would tell me they liked my stories — I just never expected it to be Isaac!

I opened the book ...

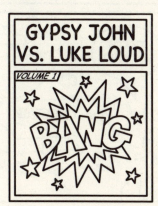

GYPSY JOHN
VS. LUKE LOUD

VOLUME 1

BANG

"That was awesome!" Isaac said, when I was finished. "I think Gypsy John is stronger than Superman!"

I laughed, because I wasn't so sure about that! "Did you really like it?" I asked him.

Isaac nodded and clapped his hands together. "You should show it to everyone else in class," he said. "They'd think it was brilliant, too!"

I felt suddenly shy again. Then Isaac mimed the way that John had taken Luke's megaphone. He repeated John's line, "'I think you've lost your voice!' Ha! Take that, Luke Loud!"

I realised that Isaac really had enjoyed hearing about Gypsy John. I had shown my comic to someone else for the first time, and they thought it was awesome.

Maybe other people would like to read it, too — one day!

Monday 29th September. 8:00 p.m.

Today was one of the best days ever! I usually head straight home after school and sit in the cook-hut listening to my cousins talking about the days they had. But not today! Today, I couldn't wait to tell everybody all about my day.

I got to school early again so I could draw more Gypsy John adventures. I normally hunch over my book while drawing so no one can see. Today, though, I sat up straight so that anyone could see it if they wanted to. I wasn't shy about my drawings anymore.

The first classmates to arrive were Amelia and Grace, two girls from the village. They walked in just before 8:30 and sat down at their desks. They didn't glance at my comic book. They didn't look at me, or say 'hello'.

Other kids started arriving, and soon loads of my classmates were gathered around Amelia's desk. They started talking about *Blind Trust*, a TV gameshow where contestants make their way through a maze while their best friend gives directions. I slumped back in my chair, because I hadn't seen it. I couldn't join in their conversation.

I looked back down at my book, right at a picture I had drawn of Gypsy John. It reminded me of what had happened on Friday — how I had talked to Isaac about my comic. Gypsy John wouldn't be shy, so I decided that I wouldn't be, either.

"I've heard that show's really cool," I said. Amelia and the others fell silent and turned round to stare at me. My ears started burning again. I was worried they were going to be mean and ask why I was butting into their conversation.

Grace smiled and nodded. "It's the best!" she said. "I want to be a contestant on it. I think I'd be good!"

Amelia shook her head. "I'd be OK with giving directions," she said. "But I would <u>not</u> go in the maze!" Then she looked right at me and asked, "What did you do over the weekend, Jack?"

Now my cheeks were getting hot as well. *Oh no,* I thought. *Don't feel shy!* "I went for a couple of walks with my cousins, in the orchard near our caravans."

Amelia pointed at herself and Grace. "We went to the adventure playground in the village. It was fun."

"But scary sometimes," Grace put in.

"You should come along next week," Amelia said. "I think lots of us are going."

I said, "Cool," like it was cool — and it was! I started feeling silly about how nervous I'd been!

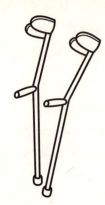

Everyone went quiet as Mr Hardy came into the class. Isaac was right behind him, walking on crutches and wobbling like he wasn't used to them. "Be careful, Isaac," Mr Hardy said.

"I will," Isaac replied as he made his way to his desk, the one next to mine. He smiled at me as he sat down. "Hi, Jack." It was the first time he had said 'hi' to me in class.

I asked how he was feeling.

"Much better now that I can come back to school," he said. "I finished reading all my football magazines by the end of Saturday, and I was very bored for all of Sunday. I wish you'd left your comic book behind. I really wanted to read more Gypsy John adventures!"

"I'll show you the next one when it's finished," I said. "I've got some wicked ideas."

"Can't wait!" Isaac said, smiling. I smiled back. I wasn't waiting for him to tell me he was only joking. I knew that he meant it.

We had maths in the morning. Mr Hardy said we would be doing addition. He asked Grace to add 226 and 113. I looked at Isaac, expecting him to jump in with an answer, like usual, but he didn't.

"339," Grace said.

"Well done, Grace," Isaac said, as Mr Hardy gave her a thumbs-up. He started to ask Amelia a different question, but I was still trying to work out how Grace got 339 from 226 and 113.

I couldn't do it.

I started to stick my hand up, then changed my mind. I didn't want to slow Mr Hardy down. I didn't want anyone to laugh at me because I couldn't do a sum that they all thought was simple. I definitely didn't want Mr Hardy to call my parents into school again ...

Then I remembered what Dad told me last week: "Some people need a bit of help at school, and that's OK."

I stuck my hand up before I could change my mind again. "I'm sorry, Mr Hardy, but can you explain how Grace got 339, please?" I cringed and waited for my classmates to laugh.

But no one did. Mr Hardy showed me how to make the sum simple, like this:

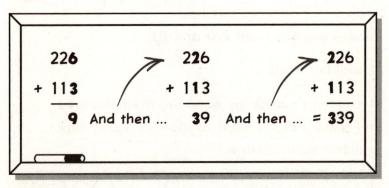

"Does that makes sense?" Mr Hardy asked.

"It does," I said, smiling. I had spoken up when I didn't understand something, and nobody had laughed at me!

As soon as I got back to the camp after school, I ran to the cook-hut. Mum, Dad and Nanny were by the fire.

"Slow down, chavvie*!" Nanny said, when she saw me running.

"I spoke up in class when I didn't understand something!" I told them. Mum hugged me and said that was brilliant news.

"Didn't I tell you it was OK to ask for help?" Dad said.

"And there's more," I said, excitedly. "Isaac read my comic, and he thinks it's brilliant!"

"I'm not surprised," Nanny said. "I bet you get your talent from <u>my</u> nan. She was a famous Gypsy storyteller, a <u>long</u> time ago."

"Really? You've got to tell me all about her later," I said, as I was running backwards towards my caravan to write in my diary. Now I've done that, I'm really excited to jot down some new ideas for Gypsy John's adventures so that I can show them to my friend Isaac.

* 'Chavvie' = 'child' or 'kid'.

Now answer the questions ...

1 What's the name of the superhero character Jack has created?

2 What does the word 'lair' mean in the phrase 'he can shatter the windows of John's caravan lair just by shouting' (page 12)?

3 Explain why Jack's face got hot when Isaac told him they didn't need any more football players (page 17).

4 What happened when Jack went over to Isaac's to take him his exercise books?

5 What did you think would happen when Jack went around to Isaac's again to get his comic book back?

6 How did the relationship between Jack and Isaac change between Jack's two visits to his house?

7 How does the word 'slumped' add to the meaning of this sentence on page 34: 'I slumped back in my chair, because I hadn't seen it.'?

8 What do you think about the way Jack behaved in the story? Would you have done anything differently?